I0813914
This book belongs to
and I am finding out
about God

Published by Candle Books
an imprint of
SPCK Group
Studio 101, The Record Hall
16-16A Baldwins Gardens. EC1N 7RJ London

ISBN 978 1 78128 275 5
e-ISBN 978 1 78128 311 0
Pack ISBN 978 1 78128 472 8

First edition 2016

A catalogue record for this book is available
from the British Library

Printed and bound in England,
April 2025

Would you like to know about God?

by Tim Dowley

Illustrated by Eira Reeves

Who is God?

The Bible tells us about God.

It has stories about people long ago who believed in God.

How old is God?

Before the world was made,
God existed.

God made the world.

He made the sun, moon, and stars.

What does God look like?

No one knows!

But the Bible tells us a lot about him.

God is like a mother bird,
who looks after her chicks.

He is like a strong rock,
where we can be safe from danger.

What does God do?

God looks after our world.
He's in charge of the sun,
the wind, and the rain.

God knows about
everything that happens.

Even when bad things happen,
God takes care of us.

God is good.

God loves us.

And God forgives us.

God is close to us and helps us.

God cares for everyone

– especially those who have
no one else to help them.

Can we talk to God?

We speak to God when we pray.

We can be safe in his love forever.
God is for always.
He never changes!